Spotlight on Kids Can Code

What Is
USER EXPERIENCE DESIGN?

Patricia Harris

PowerKiDS press
New York

Published in 2018 by The Rosen Publishing Group, Inc.
29 East 21st Street, New York, NY 10010

Copyright © 2018 by The Rosen Publishing Group, Inc.

All rights reserved. No part of this book may be reproduced in any form without permission in writing from the publisher, except by a reviewer.

First Edition

Editor: Theresa Morlock
Book Design: Michael J. Flynn
Interior Layout: Rachel Rising

Photo Credits: Cover kali9/E+/Getty Image; pp. 1, 3–24 (coding background) Lukas Rs/Shutterstock.com; p.5 garagestock/Shutterstock.com; p. 7 CandyBox Images/Shutterstock.com; p.9 Monkey Business Images/Shutterstock.com; pp.11,17 Rawpixel.com/Shutterstock.com; p.13 Lukas Gojda/Shutterstock.com; p.15 (top) ArthurStock/Shutterstock.com; p.15 (bottom) https://commons.wikimedia.org/wiki/File:MMG_-_Don_Norman_-_5552663659.jpg; p.18 Yeamake/Shutterstock.com; p.19 Benny Marty/Shutterstock.com; p.21 Denys Prykhodov/Shutterstock.com; p.22 Africa Studio/Shutterstock.com

Cataloging-in-Publication Data
Names: Harris, Patricia.
Title: What is user experience design? / Patricia Harris.
Description: New York : PowerKids Press, 2018. | Series: Spotlight on kids can code | Includes index.
Identifiers: ISBN 9781508155218 (pbk.) | ISBN 9781508155096 (library bound) | ISBN 9781508154266 (6 pack)
Subjects: LCSH: Web site development–Juvenile literature. | Web sites–Design–Juvenile literature.
Classification: LCC TK5105.888 H37 2018 | DDC 006.7–dc23

Manufactured in the United States of America

CPSIA Compliance Information: Batch #BS17PK: For Further Information contact Rosen Publishing, New York, New York at 1-800-237-9932

Contents

User Experience Design.................4
Understanding Users...................6
Ease of Use...........................8
Measuring Effectiveness..............10
Measuring Pleasantness...............12
UX in the Design Process.............14
UX Careers...........................18
No Easy Task.........................22
Glossary.............................23
Index................................24
Websites.............................24

User Experience Design

Have you ever opened a new app or program and learned to use it quickly and easily? Being able to learn a new program quickly is a sign of excellent user experience, or UX, design. UX design focuses on a user's interaction with a product. It's the work that makes someone's use of **software** or a web page the best it can be. If a product is designed to be pleasant and easy to use and helps someone achieve what they want to do effectively, the user's experience will be better.

UX design is very important to software and websites. It's also important to **hardware** and any special products that allow users to **interface** with hardware and software, such as game controllers. How does a UX designer create a product that will give a user an excellent experience?

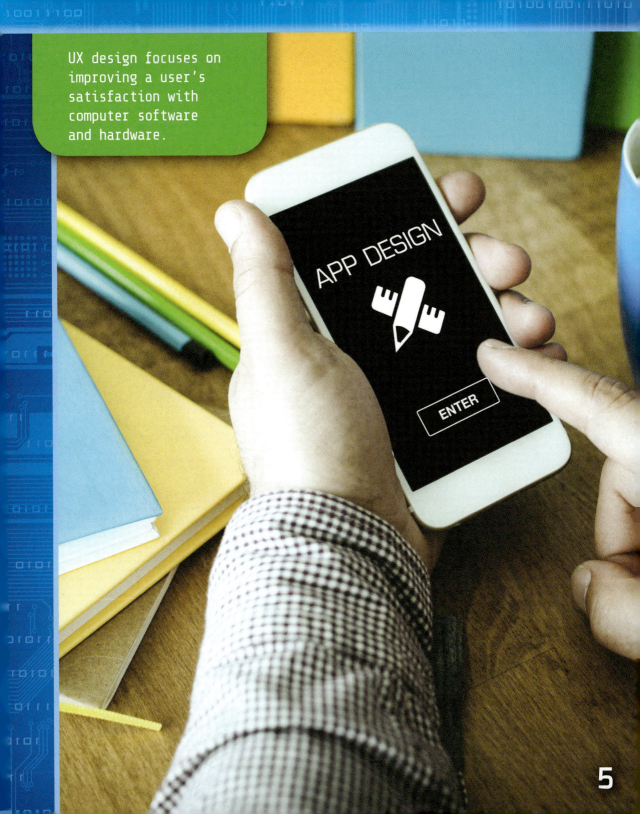

UX design focuses on improving a user's satisfaction with computer software and hardware.

Understanding Users

UX designers need to understand **technology** and know what actions must be completed to use software and hardware. Even more importantly, they need to be able to understand users. Understanding users involves thinking about how users will **relate** to the designs presented to them.

Perception, or the way a person sees or understands something, varies from person to person. For example, when two people see a dog, they might pay attention to different things. One person may say, "That dog is yellow." Another might say, "That dog has a long tail." It's easy to understand that people see the same things in different ways. A program that may seem easy to one person may seem difficult to another. A good UX designer makes a product that's **accessible** to any user. Getting inside a user's head is not an easy task.

Different people may perceive the same thing in **unique** ways. UX designers need to think about how different people will see the same product.

Ease of Use

UX designers need to create software designs that are easy to use. To do that, UX designers need to know what users want to achieve with the software. Designers need to think about what users will see as an acceptable amount of work to reach their goal. They need to make sure that users believe the software will help them reach their goal.

UX designers need to do research with users. Designers must ask questions about what goals the users have. Designers observe the actions that users do to complete their tasks and ask them why they choose to use those actions. Understanding more about users helps UX designers make software that's easy to use and helps users achieve a goal as **efficiently** as possible.

Breaking the Code

While both UX and user interface (UI) designers work on creating easy-to-use applications, they each bring a different viewpoint to the creative process. UX designers collect data from and about users. UI designers focus on the elements that the users see as they use the software to accomplish what they want to do. These elements include the **font** that is used, the color scheme, and familiar icons.

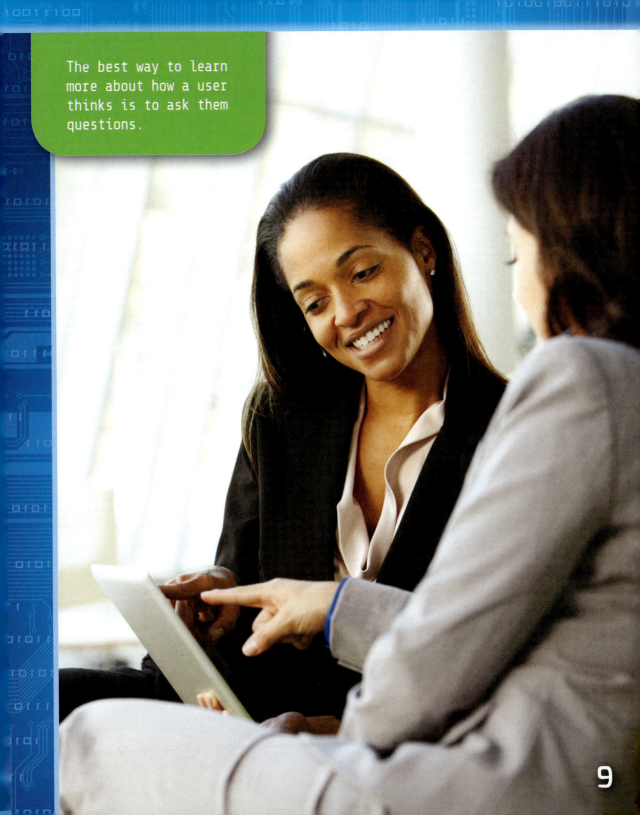

The best way to learn more about how a user thinks is to ask them questions.

Measuring Effectiveness

When UX designers have users test programs, not all users complete the task they're supposed to do on the software. When measuring the program's efficiency, it's important to include the users who don't complete the task. These users are an important part of determining the completion rate.

Completion rate refers to the percentage of users that finish a task. Completion rate is calculated by dividing the number of users who finished the task by the total number of users and then multiplying that number by 100.

If users don't complete a task, it shows that the program isn't as easy to use as it should be. The completion rate helps UX designers determine the effectiveness of a program. Counting the number of errors users make when using the program is another way to measure its effectiveness.

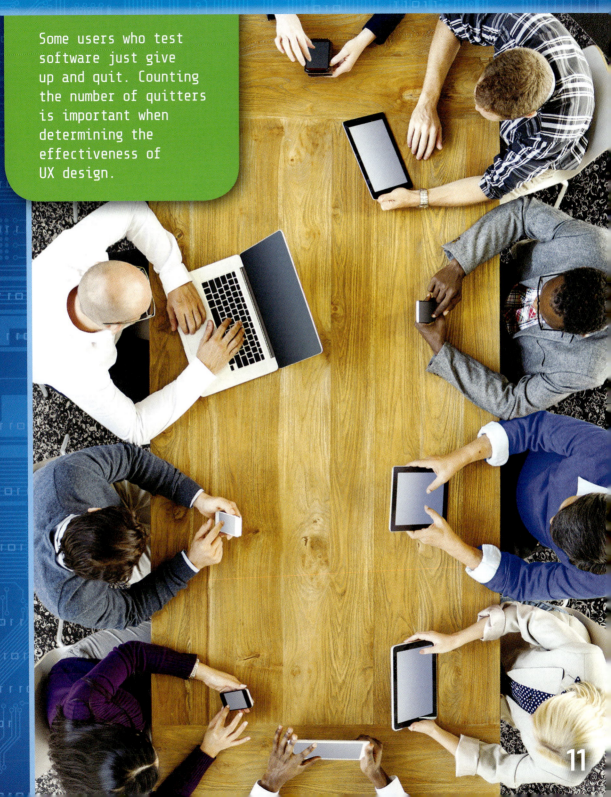

Some users who test software just give up and quit. Counting the number of quitters is important when determining the effectiveness of UX design.

Measuring Pleasantness

A program's pleasantness can't be measured by asking just one question or collecting data on the completion rate. To determine a program's pleasantness, UX designers must ask users if they feel that the program is trustworthy. They might also ask how likely a user would be to reuse the program. They're also interested if users found the program attractive to look at.

The SUPR-Q is a survey that was designed to measure how users perceive programs. The SUPR-Q uses several questions to measure pleasantness and usability.

It can be difficult to measure pleasantness. Sometimes it's easier to measure the lack of dissatisfaction. If users must stop and think about the program, it's probably something unpleasant that has caught their attention. Anything unpleasant makes the experience less enjoyable for users.

SUPR-Q is just one of the many surveys designed to measure pleasantness and usability.

13

UX in the Design Process

How does UX fit into the overall process of designing programs? There are three ways of describing how UX fits into creating software: UX is UI, UX is a job, and UX is a process.

UI is short for user interface, or the means by which a user and computer interact. UX can be seen as UI because elements of UX design are used whenever a user interface is created. Everyone who works on a project plans relationships between the product and the user. In this way, UX is a way of thinking about how to develop the best relationships between user and computer.

The second way of viewing UX is to think of it as a job. This view says a UX designer is a person who designs for the effectiveness of a program or website.

The term "user experience" was coined by designer Donald Norman in the 1990s.

The third way of looking at UX is to view it as a process. Paul Hershey is a UX professional who created a five-step UX process.

The steps are:
1. Preplanning
2. Exploration
3. Design
4. Quality
5. Feedback

Step one is to learn about the users and their task. Step two is to figure out the requirements for the software, considering the user, the company goals, and the market. This step can involve sketching, considering information design, and creating **prototypes**. Step three is to do **mock-ups** and get **feedback** from users. Step four is to check for efficiency and errors made when using the software. This step may include beta testing. Step five is to collect feedback on the software after its release to see how it's working in the real world.

A beta test is an early release of software to a limited number of users for the purpose of testing and receiving feedback. Beta versions of software are sometimes called "demos," which is short for "demonstrations."

UX Careers

A UX designer's job is very important to the whole design of a new software product. Their job is to focus the entire design team on creating an easy-to-use, effective, and pleasant product. UX designers must be able to make the design requirements clear to the developers who will create the final product. Even more importantly, UX designers need to be able to understand a user's point of view. They need to clearly understand how the product will be used, the skill level of the typical user, and what users might like to see in a product.

To be successful, UX designers need to be curious about people. They need to ask questions about why people do things and the way they do them. UX designers need to be empathetic, which means being sensitive to other peoples' emotions.

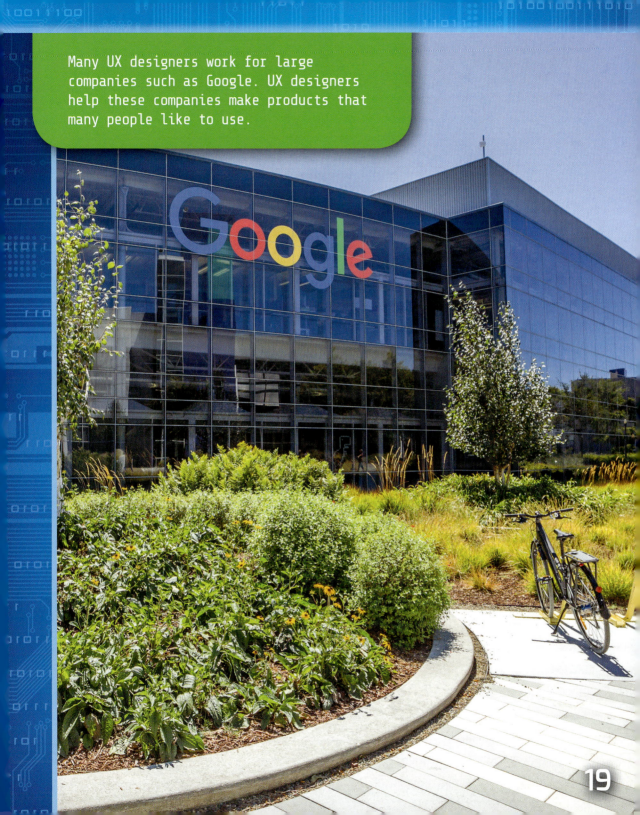

Many UX designers work for large companies such as Google. UX designers help these companies make products that many people like to use.

UX designers must have strong communication skills. They need to interact with people on many different levels using many different forms of media. Communication takes place in person and online through chats, e-mail, and text messages. In addition to interacting with users, UX designers interact with project managers, software developers, and other designers, particularly UI designers. While UX designers usually do not have to be programmers, they must understand how programmers work.

UX designers have many skills that help them work with the many people on design teams. UX designers most often enter jobs with experience working on software projects. They may have worked as researchers, visual designers, software testers, or in almost any job in which they helped create software. They need to have some understanding of the software creation process. That will help them communicate better with their team.

UX designers frequently update websites such as Facebook to improve effectiveness, ease of use, and pleasantness.

21

No Easy Task

UX design isn't easy! When trying to create a pleasant program, it's important to remember that what may please one person may displease another. What pleases a certain user at first may displease them in the future. In this way, UX designers must be careful when designing programs for pleasantness. Ease of use and effectiveness are design concerns that may be easier to achieve.

Although some programs may be pleasant and effective at first, over time they can become unpopular. In the technological world, where things change very quickly, designs can become out of date unless changes are made often. People can lose interest in even the best programs if they're outdated. UX designers must be willing to put in a lot of work to keep their programs fresh and appealing to use.

Glossary

accessible: Easy to use or understand.

efficient: Done in the quickest, best way possible.

feedback: Information about reactions to a product or the performance of a task, used as a basis for improvement.

font: The style of lettering or characters.

hardware: The physical parts of a computer system, such as wires, hard drives, keyboards, and monitors.

interface: To interact or connect with something.

mock-up: A model used for experimenting.

prototype: A first model of something from which other models will be developed.

relate: To connect with something.

software: Programs that run on computers and perform certain functions.

technology: A method that uses science to solve problems and the tools used to solve those problems.

unique: One of a kind.

Index

B
beta testing, 16, 17

C
careers, 18
communication, 20
completion rate, 10, 12

F
Facebook, 21

G
Google, 18, 19

H
hardware, 4, 5, 6
Hershey, Paul, 16

M
mock-ups, 16

N
Norman, Donald, 14

P
pleasantness, 12, 13, 21, 22
programmers, 20
project managers, 20
prototypes, 16

S
software, 4, 5, 6, 8, 10, 11, 14, 16, 17, 18, 20
software developers, 18, 20
SUPR-Q, 12, 13
survey, 12, 13

U
user interface, 14
user interface design, 8, 20

W
websites, 4, 14

Websites

Due to the changing nature of Internet links, PowerKids Press has developed an online list of websites related to the subject of this book. This site is updated regularly. Please use this link to access the list: www.powerkidslinks.com/skcc/ued